The Insider's Guide to Protecting Your Family from Irresponsible Drivers In Missouri and Kansas

BUYING CAR INSURANCE

LAW OFFICE OF
KEVIN J. MCMANUS

Kevin J. McManus
Law Office of Kevin J. McManus
1100 Main Street, Suite 2600
Kansas City, MO 64105
www.KevinMcManusLaw.com

1st Edition

Published by the Law Office of Kevin J. McManus

Printed in the United States of America.

ISBN 978-0-692-12790-2
$16.95

Read Inside to Learn How to Protect You and Your Family from Irresponsible Drivers in Missouri and Kansas.

Find answers to critical questions on how to buy vehicle insurance coverage, including:

- **What insurance is required by law in Missouri and Kansas?**
- **If you are injured in an accident, how can you prevent your health insurance company from taking all the money and leaving you with nothing?**
- **How can you protect yourself and your family under your own car insurance policy even if the other driver has little or no insurance?**
- **What must you ask your agent to get this protection and how can you confirm the level of coverage?**
- **Why doesn't the insurance company share with you what is in this book?**

CAR AND TRUCK ACCIDENTS ARE THE #1 CAUSE OF ACCIDENTAL DEATH AND DISABILITY IN THE UNITED STATES

In 2015, there were approximately 6,296,000 motor vehicle crashes in the United States that were reported to police. The number of unreported crashes is significantly higher.

Of reported crashes, 2.443 million people were injured and 35,485 people were killed. That means about 102 people died every day in vehicle crashes in the United States which is one death every 20 minutes. The financial cost of these crashes was approximately $250 billion.

In recent years, the number of motor vehicle crashes and deaths has been trending upwards. While cars are being made safer, text messaging and the increased use of cell phones has likely been a factor as distracted driving continues to rise.

NEARLY 30% OF DRIVERS CARRY NO CAR INSURANCE

According to a recent study by Insurance Research Council (IRC), roughly 1 in 7 drivers have no insurance (are uninsured) in the United States. In some states, the percentage of uninsured drivers is nearly 30%. Also, most states have minimum insurance requirements that are extremely low. In Missouri and Kansas, the minimum insurance required for injury claims is $25,000.

WITH SO MANY UNINSURED AND UNDERINSURED DRIVERS, RESIDENTS IN MISSOURI & KANSAS
ARE AT ENORMOUS RISK WITH INSUFFICIENT COVERAGE.

WHO WROTE THIS BOOK AND WHY?

Thank you for requesting this book on how to purchase car insurance in Kansas and Missouri. I hope this book will provide you with good, basic information about automobile insurance so you can learn how to protect yourself and your family from irresponsible drivers.

Let me be clear: **I do not sell insurance**. My only interest is to share information I have acquired from my law practice so you can make the best decision for you and your family and avoid pitfalls and surprises later.

For many years, I have represented individuals in Missouri and Kansas who have been injured in car accidents. Time and time again, I have reviewed a client's insurance policy and found coverage that is less than what the client believed he or she purchased long ago. Believe me – you do not want to find out that the insurance protection you thought you had is not there when you need it most.

I have good news for you. By getting this book, you have taken the first step to ensure that this will not happen to you. You could have ignored this opportunity and continued on like most consumers. Instead, you now have a comprehensive resource on how to buy car insurance to protect you and your family.

After reviewing this book, you will know what type and level of insurance coverage will provide you and your family the best protection. If you have questions about insurance or a legal issue, please feel free to call our office. My hope is that you will look to us for help when you need it. We are excited to serve you.

Sincerely,

Kevin McManus

www.KevinMcManusLaw.com

About Kevin McManus:

- Attorney representing individuals in car, motorcycle & truck accidents
- Named "Best of the Bar" by *Kansas City Business Journal*
- Recognized by *SuperLawyers* Magazine as a "Rising Star"
- Licensed in Kansas and Missouri with active trial practices in both states
- Graduate of Roberts Trial Academy, Kansas City Metropolitan Bar Association
- Member of City Council in Kansas City, Missouri, with extensive knowledge and experience in transportation and infrastructure laws
- Former member of the Missouri House of Representatives and recipient of legislative award from the Missouri Bar for contributions to civil justice issues
- Author of numerous consumer books and reports

The Dreaded Late-Night Phone Call

Imagine for a moment what it is like to be in the shoes of one of our clients.

Late one night, you are awakened by the dreaded phone call. The police officer tells you that your loved one (husband, wife, or child) has been seriously injured in a car crash. A drunk driver has changed your life forever.

When you arrive at the hospital you find your loved one on life support. He or she has suffered a brain injury and several broken bones. The doctors tell you that the badly crushed left foot may have to be amputated.

After several long and grueling nights in the hospital, your loved one awakens from the coma, but now the recovery begins. The next stop is a rehabilitation center where your loved one will have to relearn how to walk, talk, and do all the daily things we take for granted. It may be many months or even years before he/she can return to work.

The medical costs pile-up:

- $10,964 for every day spent in intensive care
- $3,450 for the rest of the days in the hospital
- $1,234 for every day spent in the rehabilitation center
- Thousands of dollars for future medical care, including multiple surgeries
- Thousands more in lost wages

The medical costs and expenses continue to pile up. At the same time, your loved one is unable to work to help pay the bills.

Total Medical Bills & Lost Wages: $194,591.34

What Will You Do?

As days pass, you become increasingly concerned about the unbelievably high medical bills. There must be an easy answer. The drunk driver's insurance company will certainly pay the medical bills, won't it? He is required to have enough insurance for that – right?

WRONG!

The problems have just begun. Unfortunately, Missouri law only requires drivers to carry $25,000 in liability coverage and that is not enough to cover your loved one's bills. So how much insurance, if any, did the drunk driver have?

After investigating this for you, we find out that the drunk driver only had the minimum insurance required by law: $25,000 to cover all the medical bills, lost wages, and pain and suffering caused by this accident. "That's not surprising," we say, "because a substantial number of people in Missouri and Kansas carry the **bare minimum** in car insurance."

What's even worse, there's more bad news!

The medical bills were partially paid through a health insurance plan of your loved one's employer. The employer had a self-insured health care plan that is governed by a federal law, known as "ERISA". The language in the plan states that, "If we pay medical bills for an accident and you make a recovery, then we are reimbursed first for all amounts we paid before you receive a dime."

This means that, even if we get money from this drunk driver's insurance, the employer's health insurance company is legally entitled to be paid back before you receive a dime.

You may ask: What about suing the drunk driver?

We advise you that it is unlikely that you will recover anything against him personally beyond the insurance policy. He is unemployed and has little to no assets. After all, he was not responsible enough to purchase adequate insurance in the first place! Any judgment against him will likely not be collectible.

Do You Know the Answer to This Question?

We then ask you the question almost none of our clients can answer: "How much Uninsured/Underinsured coverage did **you** buy to protect yourself in this situation?"

Like most consumers, you have no idea how important this coverage is.

We review the declarations page of the policy to see how much underinsurance coverage you have.

Unfortunately, we find that your policy contains the precise amount of underinsurance coverage required under Missouri law: **NONE**.

That's right. Missouri law does not require Missouri drivers to purchase underinsurance coverage.[1]

You had no idea that you needed this coverage, but it is exactly what is needed in this situation. Underinsurance provides additional coverage when the party who caused the accident (i.e. the drunk driver) has an inadequate amount of insurance.

In this situation, if you had underinsured coverage, your insurance company would pay for your damages up to the limits of the underinsured coverage you purchased after you collect the entire amount of the drunk driver's insurance.

[1] As noted later in this book, Kansas law requires drivers to carry $25,000 in both uninsured and underinsured coverage. While this is better than Missouri, it is still woefully insufficient for the reasons discussed in this book.

Why didn't you know this?

We blame insurance companies and agents for not thoroughly explaining and urging you to buy the most important insurance protection available.

They don't tell you, so we will in this book.

What is Insurance?

When you buy insurance, you have a contract between the insurance company and you. You pay the premiums, and the company agrees to protect you – even from drunk drivers with little or no insurance.

We cannot put all the blame on insurance companies for producing policies that no one understands. Much of the language in a car insurance policy is required by law. Insurance policies in Missouri and Kansas do not vary much from company to company.

There are two major parts of your policy that you must understand: ***liability*** coverage and ***uninsured/underinsured*** motorist (UM/UIM) coverage. There are many other kinds of coverage available but ***liability*** and ***UM/UIM*** coverage are the most important parts of the policy to protect you and your family.

Liability Insurance

Liability insurance provides coverage to you if you cause a wreck and hurt another person. The **liability** coverage you have protects the person you injured. The insurance company will defend you (including hiring an attorney for you if you are sued) and will pay the injured person up to the limits of the **liability** coverage you purchased.

Uninsured / Underinsured Coverage

If you have **Uninsured** (UM) / **Underinsured** (UIM) motorist coverage and a driver who has no insurance or not enough insurance hurts you, then your insurance company will pay for your damages up to the limits of the UM or UIM coverage you purchased. Since the other driver has inadequate insurance, your company pays you. Don't worry, your insurance rates cannot go up because you did nothing wrong – it is not your fault the other driver did not have enough insurance.

Uninsured (UM) Motorist coverage is very important because if you are the victim of a "hit and run" and the other driver is not caught, your UM coverage will provide you with protection.

Both UM and UIM provides you with coverage if you are injured because of the fault of another driver whether you are riding in a car, riding a bicycle or even walking as a pedestrian.

Why don't they tell you that?

Insurance companies like collecting premiums, not paying claims.

Both Missouri and Kansas currently require what is known as "$25,000 / $50,000" liability coverage. This is the minimum liability coverage required of drivers in both states. You may wonder what these two numbers mean in terms of coverage. The first number tells you what coverage is available "per person" – what the limit of coverage is for each person who is injured in an accident. The second number is the maximum coverage available to all persons injured in a single accident.

So, if you have $25,000/$50,000 coverage, each person injured in a single accident would be covered up to $25,000, but the total coverage available for the accident is only $50,000. If four people are hurt in the accident, the most any one person would be paid is

$25,000, but all four people would have to share the total of $50,000.

In this situation, if any one person's damages exceeded $25,000, or if the entire claim of all people in the accident exceeds $50,000, you could be personally responsible for what the policy did not pay.

Now Do You See Why You Should Review Your Insurance Policy?

As mentioned above, Missouri law does not require drivers to carry any **underinsurance** coverage. That's right: zero. Missouri law only requires drivers to carry $25,000/$50,000 in **uninsured** coverage.

Kansas law requires that drivers carry $25,000/$50,000 in uninsured ***and*** underinsured coverage. However, carrying the minimum level required in Kansas is still inadequate. In fact, due to a nuance in Kansas law, your minimum UIM policy may "disappear".

Kansas law gives insurance companies a "credit" for amounts already paid. The insurance company only pays for UIM if you carry a UIM policy amount over and above what was paid by the liable party. So, if the drunk driver's insurance company pays you the $25,000 under a minimum policy and you only carry a minimum UIM policy of $25,000, you recover ***nothing*** in Kansas.

That's right – your UIM policy is offset and cancelled out by the $25,000 you already received from the drunk driver's insurance. Even though you thought you had UIM coverage, this nuance in Kansas law reduces your UIM coverage to zero in this case!

How Much Uninsured/Underinsured Coverage Should You Buy?

Buy as much UM/UIM coverage as your insurance company will sell you. It's just that simple.

Insurance companies will likely offer you uninsured and/or underinsured coverage. However, they may not tell you how **CRITICAL** it is to protect you and your family. Since they don't explain why you need it, you may have thought the agent was just trying to sell you coverage that you don't need.

Regardless, you should buy the highest limit of UM/UIM coverage that you can afford.

It is important to note that ten times the insurance coverage will not result in ten times the premium increase! For as little as $50 to $100 per year, you can increase your coverage from the minimum of $25,000 to $100,000 or even $250,000. This small investment can provide you and your family with substantial additional protection.

If you have the minimum required by state law, I encourage you to call your insurance agent and ask for quotes to increase liability and UM/UIM coverage in your policies. You may be surprised by how much additional coverage you can receive for a relatively modest premium increase.

Why Doesn't My Insurance Company Make Sure I Know This?

Because UM/UIM coverage is a great deal for you, but it can cost them a lot of money.

Just look at the numbers. For a little more money each year, you can receive more UM/UIM coverage and a lot more protection for your family. While the insurance company can increase their prices, they cannot stop the proliferation of uninsured or underinsured drivers who are out on the road right now!

The insurance company wants the certainty of premiums paid with minimal exposure. By selling you the liability and UM/UIM coverage at levels **adequate** to protect you and your family, they lose this certainty and have greater exposure and risk.

It's simple math, and if you are not careful, you will be on the losing end of this equation.

That's why right now you must take action.

Before you do anything else, go find your vehicle insurance policy.

Find your policy and review the "Declarations Page." This is the page that shows the insurance coverage that you have and what each type and level of coverage costs you.

Once you have that page, if it's anything less than $1,000,000, call your agent and ask them this question: "How much will it cost to increase my insurance policy to $1,000,000 of liability and $1,000,000 of UM/UIM coverage?"

The agent may tell you that you don't need that much. Don't listen to them. They may suggest that you buy an umbrella policy instead.[2] Insist that they price you that coverage, and then ask for them to price the coverage downward at $500,000, $250,000 and $100,000.

[2] Umbrella insurance is extra liability insurance that kicks in when the liability on your basic car or home insurance policy has been exhausted.

If you want to consider an umbrella policy, ask them how much it would cost to add $1,000,000 umbrella for **both liability and underinsured/uninsured motorist coverage.** Beware: not all insurance companies offer an umbrella policy with UM coverage and you should read the policy carefully to confirm.

Once you see all the prices for the different levels, buy the most insurance that you can afford.

If you have any questions about the information in this book, please call us. We believe this subject is so important that we will waive our $350 hourly fee to help. We would be happy to look at your policy, answer questions you may have, and discuss how to increase protection for you and your family.

SAMPLE DECLARATION PAGE

THIS DECLARATIONS PAGE IS PART OF YOUR POLICY, PLEASE READ CAREFULLY

Traders Insurance Company
PO Box 34588 8916 Troost Ave Kansas City, MO 64131
816-333 6810

Policy Number Renewal of:
[redacted]

POLICY PERIOD
EFFECTIVE: 10 30 2016 12:01 AM
EXPIRATION: 04 30 2017 12:01 AM

11/17/2016 AMENDED
PERSONAL AUTO POLICY DECLARATIONS
(RENEWAL)

ENDORSEMENT:

NAMED INSURED	AGENCY NAME & ADDRESS
[redacted]	THE AHBE GROUP INC (4716295-00-01) 1614 ARMSTRONG AVE KANSAS CITY, KS 66102 (913) 499-9246

INSURED VEHICLE DESCRIPTION

Veh #	Year	Make/Model	VIN	Symbols Lia/CP/CL/Mum	State	Garaging Zip/ and Terr	Usage/ Surcharged	Age
1	1998	DODGE INTREPID	[redacted]	3/18/11/3	KS	66101	Pleasure Only / N	20
2	2002	CHEVROLET TRAILBLAZER	[redacted]	2/11/10/4	KS	66101	Pleasure Only / N	16
3	2003	CHEVROLET CAVALIER LS SPO	[redacted]	3/18/18/4	KS	66101	Pleasure Only / N	15

GARAGE ADDRESS

Veh #	Year	Make/Model	Garaging Address
1	1998	DODGE INTREPID	[redacted]
2	2002	CHEVROLET TRAILBLAZER	
3	2003	CHEVROLET CAVALIER LS SPORT	

LIENHOLDER/ADDITIONAL INTEREST

Veh #	Type	Lienholder

DRIVERS

Drv #	Name	DOB	Marital / Sex	SR-22 Filed	State Filed	Status	Points
1	[redacted]	[redacted]	[redacted]	YES	KS	Rated 2,2	6
2	[redacted]	[redacted]	[redacted]	NO		Rated 3,3	3
3	[redacted]	[redacted]	[redacted]	NO		Rated 1,1	0

CURRENT COVERAGES

Coverages	Limits Of Liability	Veh 1	Veh 2	Veh 3
Bodily Injury Liability	$25,000 per person/ $50,000 per accident	$ 125	$ 125	$ 131
Property Damage Liability	$10,000 per accident	$ 156	$ 156	$ 164
Uninsured Motorists - BI	$25,000 per person / $50,000 per accident	$ 7	$ 8	$ 8
Personal Injury Protection	Statutory	$ 54	$ 62	$ 62
24 Hour Roadside Service	V1 $100 per OccurrenceV2 $100 per OccurrenceV3 $100 per Occurrence	$ 36	$ 36	$ 36
	Vehicle Totals	$ 378	$ 387	$ 401

**<u>CREDITS/SURCHARGES APPLIED:</u> Continuous Coverage Discount,EFT Discount,Multi Car

Endorsements - form numbers of endorsements attached to policy:	
Roadside All (2010-08), TIC-10-KS (10/2006)	Vehicles Premiums $ 1,166 * SR-22 Filings $ 18 * See additional premiums below

* A Service Charge Premium of $3.00 will be charged on your down payment and each time you are invoiced for amounts due to continue your policy. We may charge you other incidental fees such as SR-22 filing fees, returned check fees and fees related to failure to timely make your premium payments. All Service Charge Premiums and other fees are fully earned.

The premium charge set forth in these declarations is based on information provided in the application. By reference the application is made a part hereof. Please verify that the information provided in the application and set forth in these declarations is accurate and notify your agent immediately of any errors.
Countersigned At Kansas City, Missouri on 11/17/2016 9:52 AM by B P Concannon III

Dec (2011/06)

This line shows the amount of uninsurance coverage. This policy is for the minimum UM coverage of $25,000. This is inadequate. Note that the cost is only $8 per vehicle. Just imagine how inexpensive it is to get much better coverage!

HOW IS OUR FIRM DIFFERENT?

We are different from most law firms. We know all our clients by their name. Our purpose is simple – to help people with their legal problems. We believe we can best do that when we know our clients as people and not just as numbers.

This philosophy and set of values guide how we do our work and the experience you will have if you hire our firm. Our goal is not to be the biggest law firm in the state. We do not rely on a high volume of cases. We do not advertise on television or in the yellow pages. We do not claim to handle every kind of legal case. We do not want to do every kind of case, and frankly, we do not need to.

We only accept a limited number of serious injury and accident cases each year. Unlike some "injury mill" firms, we do not accept cases with questionable merit or try to settle large numbers of cases for pennies on the dollar. Our paralegals and assistants do not negotiate cases with the insurance company. By limiting our practice and taking fewer cases, we are able to give each of our clients the attention and care that that they deserve, and we believe this produces better results.

We take pride in our results-driven, client-centered approach. Communication with our clients is a critical part of this. We will explain the legal process to you, answer all your questions, and keep you informed about your case.

Sometimes the advice you receive when you are considering a lawsuit is that you do not have a claim that can be won. If that is true, we will tell you. We will also tell you if we think that you are better off handling your claim without an attorney.

But, if we are your attorney, you can rest assured that you will receive our personal attention. We will aggressively represent you, keep you advised on the progress of your case, and give you straight advice on whether you should settle or go to trial.

Together, we will act as a team to decide on the best strategy to resolve your case.

WHY EXPERIENCE MATTERS

You should know that each case is different, and past results are not a guarantee of future results. For this reason, you should be very concerned if an attorney guarantees a result in your case based on a prior case they handled. Nevertheless, when selecting an attorney, you need an attorney with experience in personal injury cases, and a brief story illustrates why.

In late 2017, we were contacted by a couple injured in a serious car accident in Johnson County, Kansas. The husband was driving and his wife was riding in the front passenger seat. As he entered an intersection, another car ran a red light and struck them on the passenger side in a "T-bone" collision.

The husband was not very badly injured, but his wife was seriously injured because she was sitting where the impact occurred. She had multiple broken bones and a spinal injury. Surgery was required. Medical bills grew. They sought legal guidance.

They were referred to a criminal defense attorney who supposedly did a little personal injury on the side. It is unclear what happened next, but nearly two years after the accident, they were referred to our firm. No lawsuit had been filed. No settlement offer had been made by the insurance company.

The statute of limitations for personal injury cases in Kansas is two years. This deadline is extremely important. If you do not assert all claims you have within two years, those claims are forever barred, and you will not recover a dime.

Our office pushes our cases forward so they are resolved as soon as possible. If they cannot be resolved with a pre-suit demand, we tell our client that we need to file suit, and we prepare for trial. Typically, we will not take a case if it is even close to the statute of limitations deadline.

We explained this to the couple, but they pleaded with our office to help. After reviewing the records, we discovered the reason why the insurance company was not paying them. There was no video of the crash. The husband said he had a green light, and the other driver said he had a green light. The insurance company was using their competing statements to deny paying the person who clearly was not at fault but who was most injured: the wife. She was not driving, but she was the one most badly injured. Even worse, they were saying the husband was at fault even though he was a retired professional driver with years of training and experience in safe driving.

After discussing various options and strategies with this couple, we agreed that we would represent only the wife and that we would file suit immediately against the other driver and the husband. Why? If the insurance company was going to argue that the husband was negligent, then we needed to add him as a defendant to force both insurance companies to the table. The husband and wife understood and agreed with this approach.

Within days of our filing suit and sending a demand, **BOTH** insurance companies – for the husband and the other driver – paid policy limits to our client. Each insurance company paid a six-figure amount, which in sum was well over her medical bills. Finally, the couple finally received fair compensation for the wife's pain and suffering.

The morale of the story is simple: experience matters. You must find an attorney who has experience handling complex personal injury cases and who will investigate the facts fully and think creatively about strategies. You need to hire an attorney who will pursue your case with diligence and communicate with you every step of the way so you get the result you deserve. If you do not, you may never receive the compensation you deserve for your injuries.

WHAT OTHERS ARE SAYING

Below are some testimonials from those we have worked with in the past. As you will discover, the issues you encounter do not have to be difficult, and help is available.

"Kevin was very professional, but approachable and friendly. He kept me informed of the progress of my case, and fought for me to receive the maximum I could receive. He finished my case in a few months, after I had been waiting for two years under another attorney."

-Kathleen, Johnson County, Kansas

"Kevin McManus works hard for his clients and cares about his community. He represented me on a car accident case. Without his help, I would have been left with unpaid bills for my injuries and would never have received the compensation I deserved."

-Steve, Kansas City, Missouri

"Kevin McManus is an excellent lawyer and a wonderful person. He cares about his clients and works very hard to obtain the very best results. I have worked with Kevin on several cases and have been very impressed with his work. Kevin is an absolute pleasure to work with, and he treats everyone like family."

-Scott Shachtman, Co-counsel

"Kevin is a great lawyer who is very responsive. He is well known in the community and can handle many different types of practice areas. I fully recommend him as an attorney."

-Phyllis Norman, Referring Attorney

FREE INFORMATIONAL NEWSLETTERS

Want to know:

- How to best deal with insurance company denials?
- How to protect yourself from financial ruin?
- Legal insider tips about Kansas and Missouri law?
- How current legal issues and cases may affect you?
- Specific steps you can take to find the best lawyer for your case?
- Practical advice about buying insurance from one who does not sell insurance?

These are some of the topics that are covered monthly in our free newsletter that is available to you.

Our firm strongly believes that most legal disputes could be avoided if people had a better general knowledge about the legal system, insurance coverage, and the insurance claim process.

There is absolutely no cost or obligation to receive our newsletter, and from time to time, we run contests to give away free items!

Don't worry, this is not the boring, "canned" newsletter that most firms buy and add on their name. We write it ourselves to encourage people to pay more attention to their legal affairs.

If you later feel like you want to stop receiving our newsletter, there is a phone number in every issue that you can call to "unsubscribe."

To receive this newsletter, just photocopy this form, fill it out and e-mail or mail it to us. Email to: Newsletter@KevinMcManusLaw.com or mail to Kevin McManus, 1100 Main Street, Suite 2600, Kansas City, MO 64105.

Please send me your free legal newsletter:

Name:

____

Address:

____

City:__________ State: __________ Zip: ____________

If you would like to receive our **email** newsletter, please include your email here:

E-mail:________________________________

We do not share mail/email lists with anyone!

FREE Book for Accident Victims in Missouri and Kansas

Great news! A free book is now available for victims of car or other injury accidents in Missouri and Kansas. There is no obligation or cost with requesting this book, and you should request it today before you talk to an insurance adjuster or hire an attorney.

Copy and fill out this form and mail or e-mail this form back to us to learn:

- Who will pay my medical bills?
- Will I be paid for the time I'm losing from work?
- Should I give a recorded statement to the insurance adjuster or sign their forms?
- What do I do if the person who hit my car doesn't have car insurance?
- What if I don't make a full recovery and cannot return to work?

- How will I know if the insurance company's settlement offer is fair?
- Should I hire an attorney to represent me, and if so, how to I find the right one?

To receive this free book, just photocopy this form, fill it out and e-mail or mail it to us. Email us at: AccidentBook@KevinMcManusLaw.com or mail to Kevin McManus, 1100 Main Street, Suite 2600, Kansas City, MO 64105.

Please send me a free copy of *Crash Course: An Insider's Guide to Accident & Injury Law in Missouri & Kansas*:

Name:

____

Address:

____

City:__________ State: __________ Zip: ____________

We do not share mail lists with anyone!

Made in the USA
Monee, IL
04 November 2026

67381826R00024